Bedtime Yoga

CREATING YOUR CHAKRA RAINBOW

MIKE AND VICTORIA DOWNS

Illustrated by **Manuela Adreani**

DeVorss Publications

This book is dedicated to
remembering that the colors
of the rainbow are inside
each and every one of us.

BEDTIME YOGA

Text Copyright © 2025 by Mike and Victoria Downs
Illustrations Copyright © 2025 by Manuela Andreani

ISBN 978-087516-957-6 print
ISBN 978-0875516-958-3 ebook

First Edition, 2025

Library of Congress Control Number: 2025931498

Printed in the United States

Design by Michelle Farinella Design

DeVorss & Company, Publishers
P. O. Box 1389
Camarillo, CA 93011-1389
www.devorss.com

What is Yoga?

AN ANCIENT SYSTEM *of* PRACTICES used to achieve **wellness**

by balancing the mind and body through exercise,

meditation *(mental focus)*, and control of the

internal energies influenced by breathing patterns and emotions.

There are numerous energy points in your body call Chakras.

The word **CHAKRA** (cakra in Sanskrit) means **"wheel"**.

Each chakra is thought to be a spinning disk of energy that should stay **"open"** and aligned, as it corresponds to bundles of nerves, major organs, and areas of your energetic body that affect your emotional and physical well-being.

What are Chakras?

Some say there are 114 different chakras, but there are seven main chakras that run along your spine. Chakras have only recently become more well-known, with the growth in popularity of yoga and New Age philosophies in general. They are a complex and ancient energy system that originated in India and were first mentioned in the Vedas, ancient sacred texts of spiritual knowledge dating from 1500 to 1000 BC.

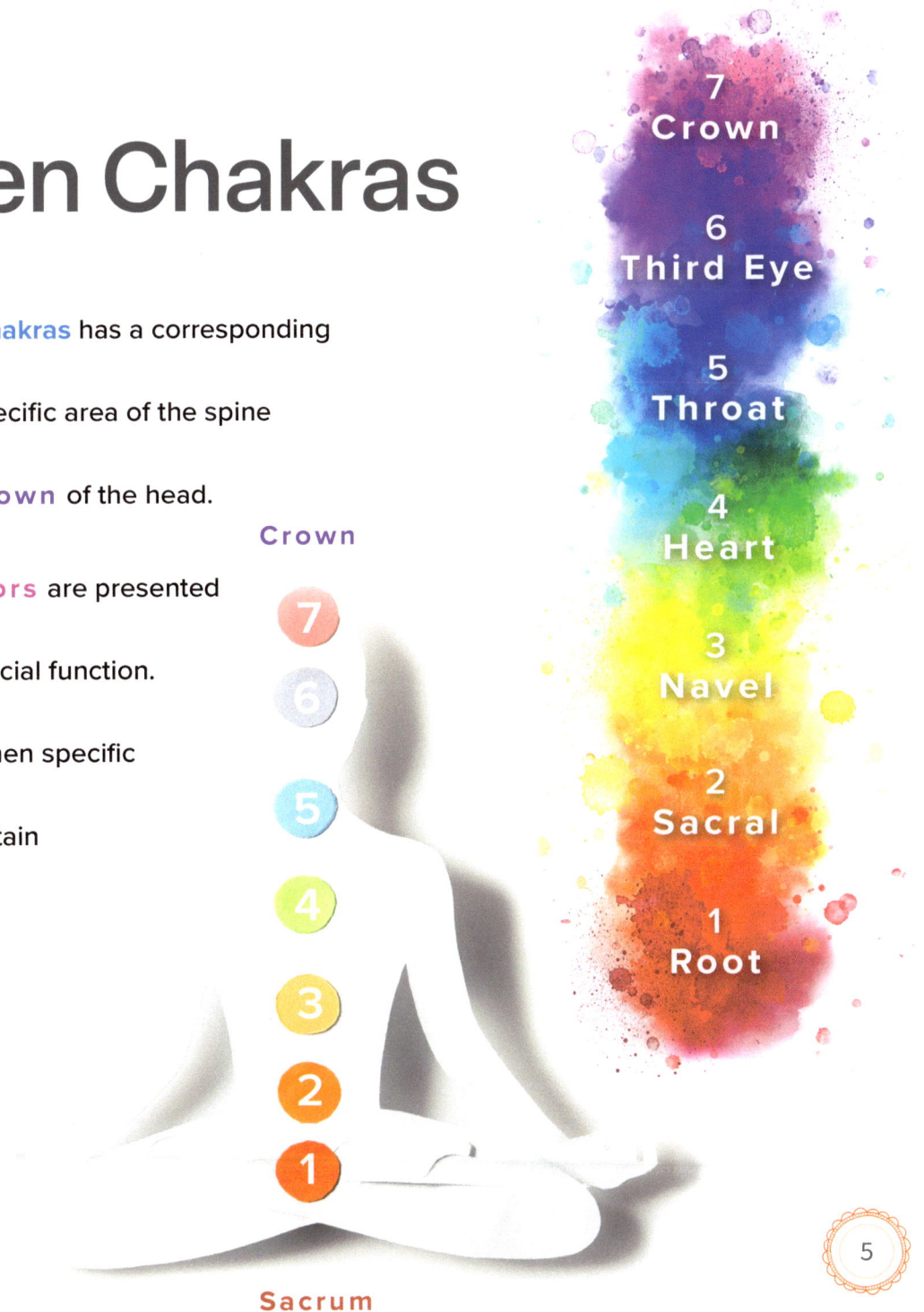

The Seven Chakras

Each of these seven main chakras has a corresponding

number, name, color, and specific area of the spine

from the Sacrum to the Crown of the head.

The seven chakras' colors are presented

here as a rainbow with a special function.

Specific yoga poses strengthen specific

chakras that help us to maintain

a physically and emotionally

balanced life . . . at any age.

Crown

7
6
5
4
3
2
1

Sacrum

7
Crown

6
Third Eye

5
Throat

4
Heart

3
Navel

2
Sacral

1
Root

5

It is important to focus on your breathing as you practice yoga poses with your child.

Breathing

The **stanza** below is for the adult/parent and child to say aloud **together** with each pose. Here is a mantra that will be simple for a child to learn. By focusing on your **breathing,** it provides the time to repeat the **mantra** and hold each **pose**.

Breathe in . . . *hussh*

deep and long

Breathe out . . . *hissh*

make it strong.

In . . . *hussh*.

Out . . . *hissh*.

Like a puffy goldfish.

Chakra rainbow start with **red,**

end with **purple,** then to **bed.**

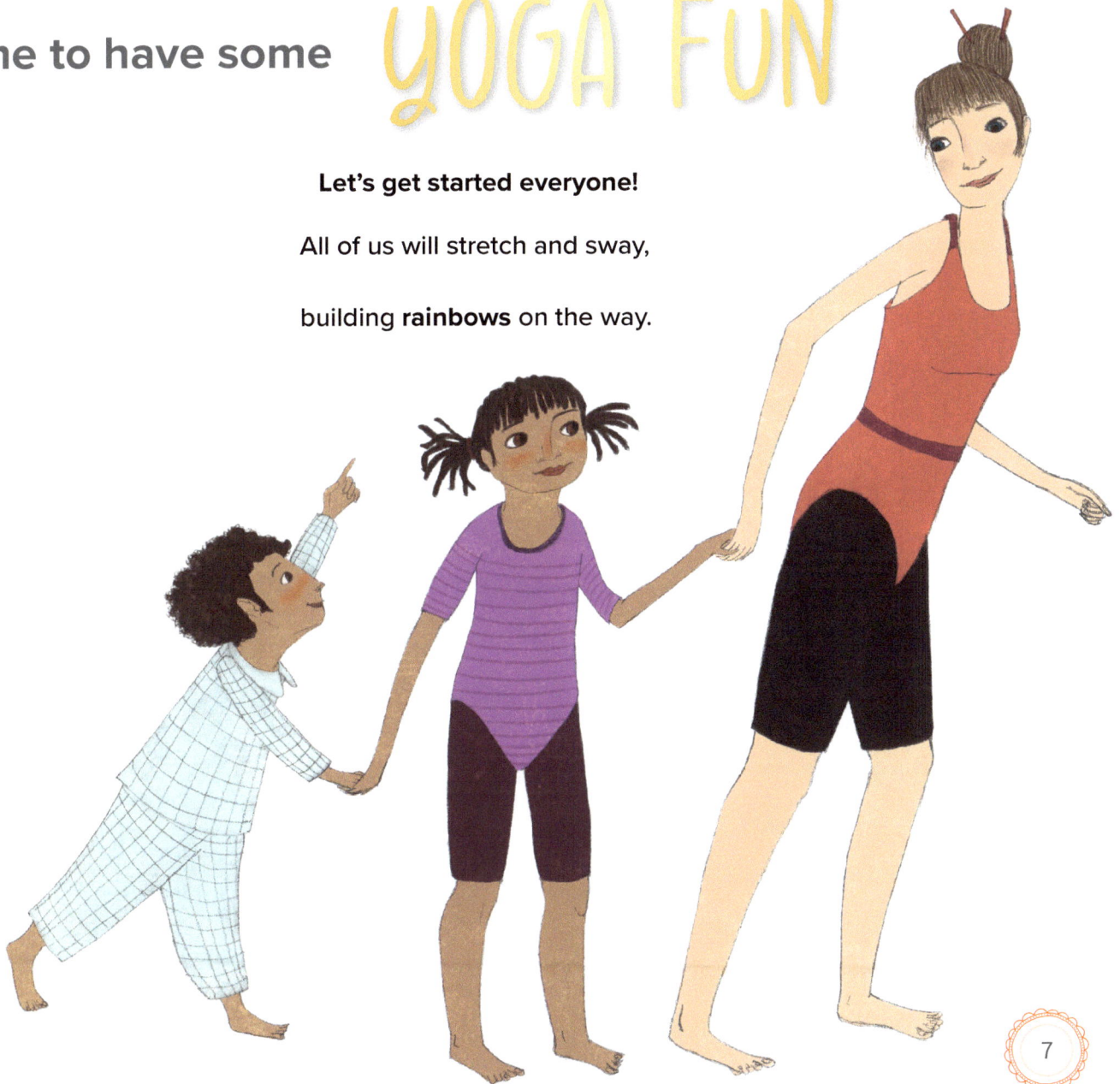

It's time to have some **YOGA FUN**

Let's get started everyone!

All of us will stretch and sway,

building **rainbows** on the way.

The 1st color of the rainbow

is **Red**,

the Root Chakra.

It makes us feel safe.

Bend your knees to start the night,
squatting with your hands in tight.

Here we learn we're safe at home,
knowing that we're not alone.

The Garland Pose

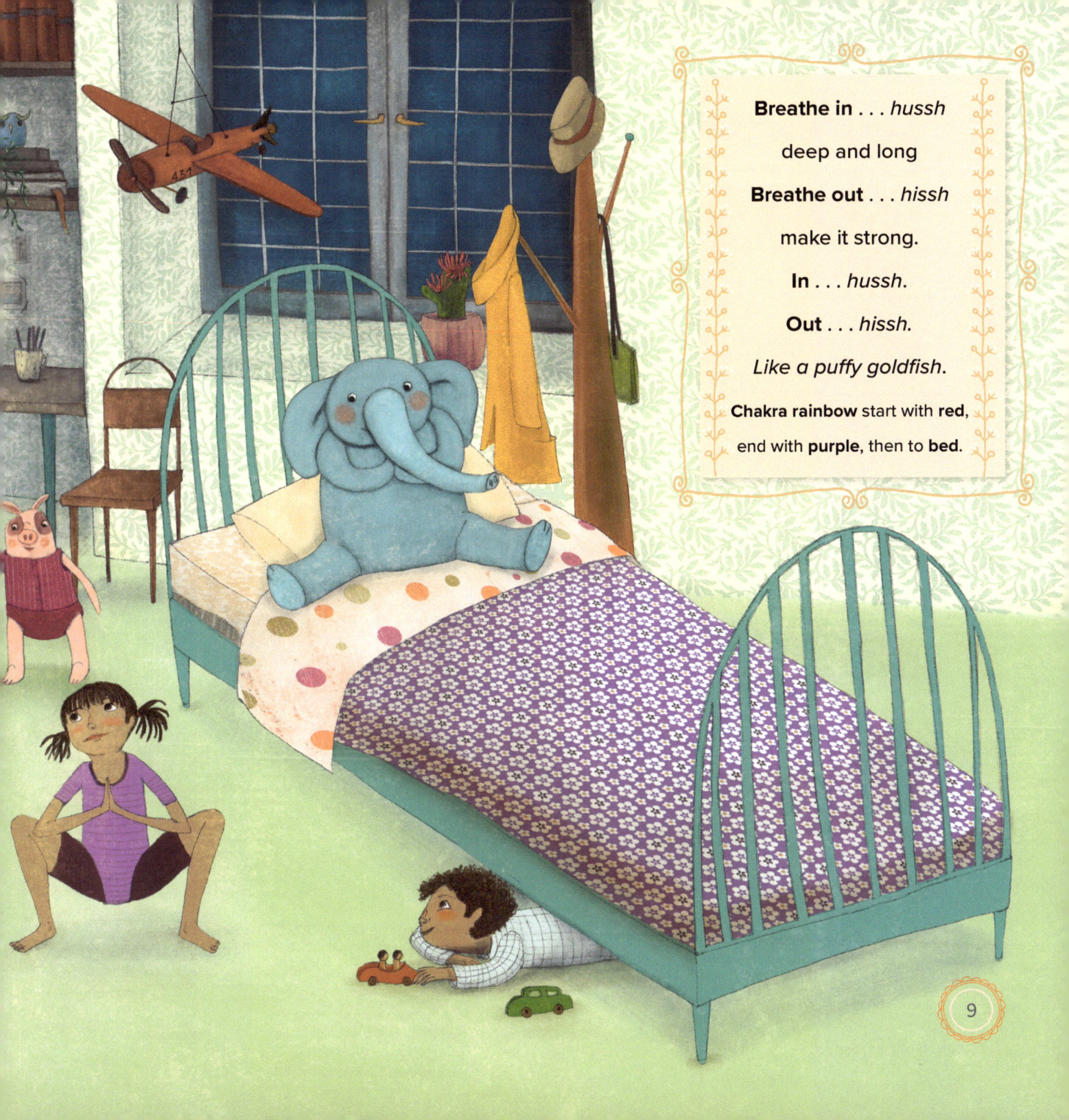

Breathe in . . . *hussh*

deep and long

Breathe out . . . *hissh*

make it strong.

In . . . *hussh.*

Out . . . *hissh.*

Like a puffy goldfish.

Chakra rainbow start with **red**,

end with **purple**, then to **bed**.

The 2nd color of the rainbow

is **Orange**,

the Sacral Chakra.

It brings happiness.

Lift your tushes. Hold them high.

Keep them pointed toward the sky.

This will bring us joy and light,

creative feelings, fresh and bright.

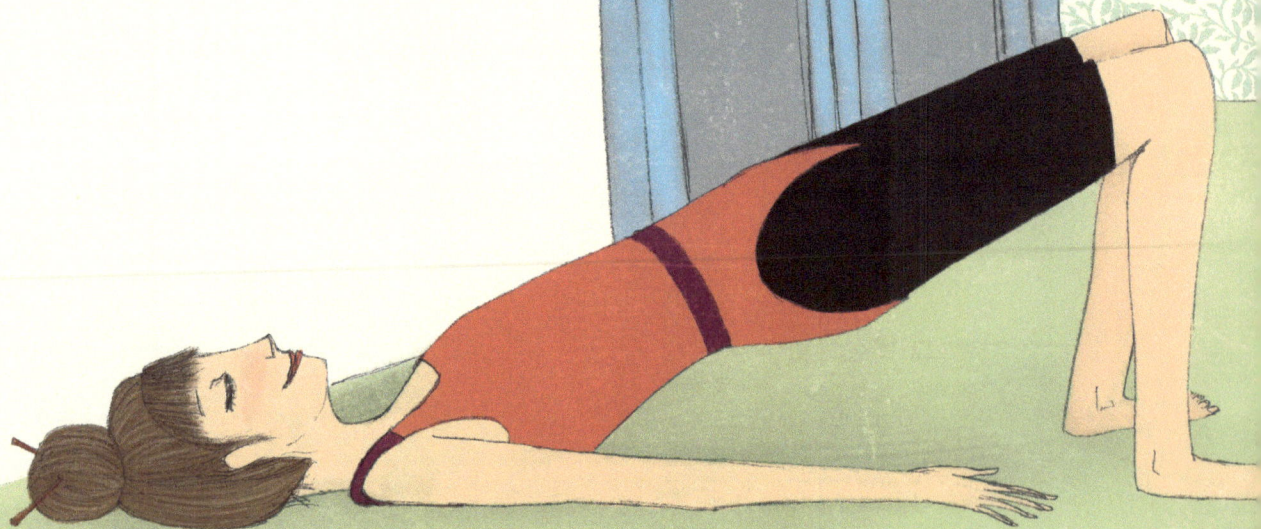

10 **The Bridge Pose**

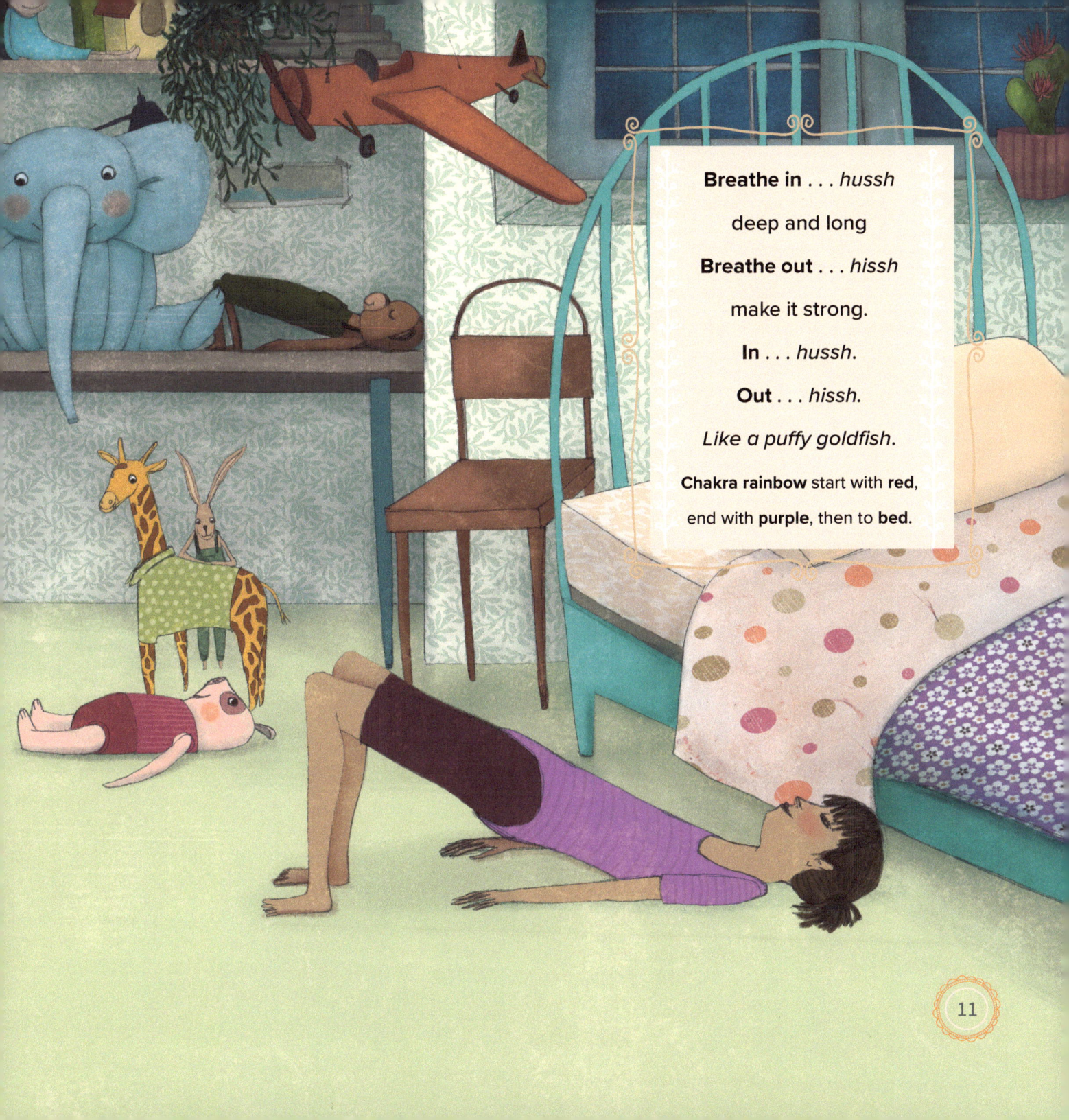

Breathe in . . . *hussh*

deep and long

Breathe out . . . *hissh*

make it strong.

In . . . *hussh.*

Out . . . *hissh.*

Like a puffy goldfish.

Chakra rainbow start with **red**,

end with **purple**, then to **bed**.

11

The 3rd color of the rainbow

is **Yellow**,

the Navel Chakra.

It helps us believe in ourselves.

Kneel slowly, that's a start.
Leaning forward, hands apart.

This makes your mind and body strong.
You'll feel at home, where you belong!

The Front Platform Pose

Breathe in . . . *hussh*

deep and long

Breathe out . . . *hissh*

make it strong.

In . . . *hussh*.

Out . . . *hissh*.

Like a puffy goldfish.

Chakra rainbow start with **red**,

end with **purple**, then to **bed**.

13

The 4th color of the rainbow
is **Green,**
the Heart Chakra.

It teaches love.

Hunching up, just like a cat,

then like a cow who's bent his back.

Wrapped in love from me and you,

learning love for others too.

14 **The Cat Cow Pose**

Breathe in . . . *hussh*

deep and long

Breathe out . . . *hissh*

make it strong.

In . . . *hussh.*

Out . . . *hissh.*

Like a puffy goldfish.

Chakra rainbow start with **red**,

end with **purple**, then to **bed**.

The 5th color of the rainbow

is **Blue**,

the Throat Chakra.

It teaches us to tell the truth.

Sitting back, with hands on knees,

stick your tongue out in the breeze.

We learn to speak up honestly

To set our hearts and spirits free.

The Lion Pose

Breathe in . . . *hussh*

deep and long

Breathe out . . . *hissh*

make it strong.

In . . . *hussh.*

Out . . . *hissh.*

Like a puffy goldfish.

Chakra rainbow start with **red**,

end with **purple**, then to **bed**.

17

The 6th color of the rainbow

is **Indigo**,

the Third Eye Chakra.

It helps us understand the world.

Find the eye you cannot see.

Touch the floor there, quietly.

Here we'll try to understand

People all throughout the land.

The Child Pose

Breathe in . . . *hussh*

deep and long

Breathe out . . . *hissh*

make it strong.

In . . . *hussh.*

Out . . . *hissh.*

Like a puffy goldfish.

Chakra rainbow start with **red**,

end with **purple**, then to **bed.**

19

The 7th color of the rainbow

is **Purple**,

the Crown Chakra.

It connects us with the universe.

Lying down, it's time to doze.

Hands beside you, stretch your toes.

Feel the universe inside.

We're all connected, far and wide.

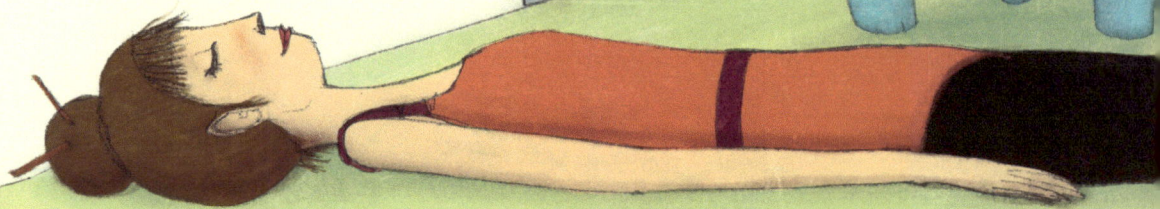

20 **The Savasana Pose**

Breathe in . . . *hussh*

deep and long

Breathe out . . . *hissh*

make it strong.

In . . . *hussh.*

Out . . . *hissh.*

Like a puffy goldfish.

Chakra rainbow start with **red**,

end with **purple**, then to **bed**.

When your

Chakra Rainbow

is full and bright,

You will feel the glow

of inner light.

As your bedtime yoga

heart now beams,

Close your eyes . . .

and have . . .

. . . sweet dreams.

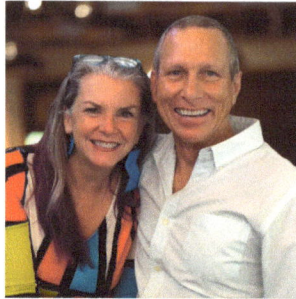

MIKE and VICTORIA DOWNS have a blended family of five amazing children! Mike is a retired commercial airline pilot and author of over 30 books, including his most recent, *A Treasure of Measures*. Victoria worked with oncology & hospice patients during her 40-year career as a registered nurse. She also explored other modalities of healing, earning certifications as a Kundalini and Trauma Informed Yoga instructor, a Healing Touch Practitioner, and an Integrative Health Coach. They now reside in Florida where you'll find them stand-up paddling or surfing the Atlantic.

www.ingramcontent.com/pod-product-compliance
Lightning Source LLC
Chambersburg PA
CBHW041959100426
42813CB00019B/2932